The Ultimate Guide To Dating And Impressing A Girl

How To Get A Girlfriend

George K.

Table of Contents

Introduction

Chapter 1 – Redefining Dating and Relationships

Chapter 2 – Preparing To Be the Right Guy

Chapter 3 – Easy Tricks to Decode Girls

Chapter 4 – Walking Your Way To Her Heart

Chapter 5 –Romantic Date Ideas to Captivate Her Heart

Conclusion

Check Out My Other Book

Before You Go

Introduction

Are you tired of being dumped? Are girls really too complex for you? Well, girls are not that complicated at all, only if you know how to interpret their language.

I want to thank you and congratulate you for downloading the book, *"The Ultimate Guide to Dating and Impressing a Girl : How To Get A Girlfriend"*.

This book provides tips and tricks on how to be the kind of guy that most girls will find irresistible. This will teach you how to be the "right guy." It will teach you the art of decoding girls so you can finally get really involved in a girl's life. You'll also learn some romantic date ideas! You can find everything you need here in this book. Date the girl you've been waiting to date for so long!

Thanks again for purchasing this book. I hope you enjoy it!

Chapter 1 – Redefining Dating and Relationships

Let me tell you a story first to just give you a preview of what you're in for.

Once upon a time, there was a rich and handsome prince sitting in his room with his friend. They were drinking the best wine in town in celebration of his brother's transition to Kinghood.

"Why is it that you never had a wife?" His friend asked in the midst of their drinking session. "You could have been a better King than your brother."

"Well," he said, "I actually tried, man." He put down his glass on the table. "You know what. I actually found the one!"

"Okay," his friend responded, baffled and with a slight grimace on his face. "What happened to her, then? Was she already married or something?"

"No. Nothing like that. You see, a few years ago, I went to a journey in looking for a great wife. My father's dying and someone has to take over. But I need to look first for a wife. You know, someone who can perfectly fit the role of a queen.

"On my first quest, I met a beautiful woman. But the thing is, she's not very smart. She is dull and has no skill in anything. So I went to my next quest and found a talented woman who has a really enchanting voice. My heart melted the moment I heard it. I was hunting in the middle of the woods that time. But then, as I followed the voice, I saw a very plain woman. She's not even half as attractive as the first one. She's not the one I'm looking for.

"In that last journey, it felt like unearthing a long lost treasure chest! But then, I actually found a wonderful woman. She's clever, kind, and beautiful! She's so perfect that I can't believe a girl like her exists. She's even a famous musical stage play actress in her town... But there's one problem..."

"What's the problem, then?"

"She's also looking for the right guy!"

The Tragedy of Modern Dating

A lot of people, both guys and girls, are hoping to fish the "right person" out of the sea of nowhere and when they do get that person, they consider themselves lucky.

Many people aren't so lucky though. The thing is, getting connected these days is easier, what with dating apps and social networks. But the thing is, in modern society, connections are superficial. It's all about quantity these days, not quantity.

And dating these days just seems to be about odds. People expose themselves to thousands, if not millions of people in social media and dating apps, and just try to make as many connections as possible, hoping that out of the millions of prospects, they'd luck out and find *the one*.

And whenever someone didn't like how it turned out, he would simply take another turn and hope for the best. But dating isn't just like that – it shouldn't be all about improving your odds by making thousands of meaningless connections.

Redefining Dating

Dating is a testing stage of two attracted people trying to know if they're fit for a relationship. It's like a transition stage from being acquaintances to an official couple. For guys, this is like their big chance in winning a girl. This is the stage where in they have to give their best shot to win a girl.

But the problem in dating is that most guys only set out their best foot to impress the girl. They fail to show who they really are. Consequently, when a nasty behavior appeared inside the relationship, it makes the girl feel like you've changed or something. It makes them think that you're not the guy they fell in love with before. But you know in yourself that it's not true. Those are just the things you didn't show her in the first stages of dating.

Dating is not just about wooing each other to win each other's heart. Rather, it's about getting to know each other deeper and better. So part of it is showing all of you, including your flaws. Although it's impossible to really show everything, it's better that both of you have an idea about each other's strength and weaknesses.

Be the Right Guy

If you want to win a girl and keep her for good, there are a lot of things you need to understand about dating and relationships. And the most important one about dating is that instead of focusing on finding the right girl, you need to focus on being the right guy first.

Even if you find the right person, if you are the "wrong" person, none of it will make any sense. Expect a painful relationship if you'll stick with that kind of set-up.

Maybe you're thinking, "I'm not really up for a serious relationship. I just want to be happy and, well, hook up a little bit." Well, you can hook up with a lot of girls in a club. They can make you happy, but if you're looking for a real connection – a real relationship, the hook-up scene is not really what you should be working on.

This book is not just about hook-ups although it would teach you tricks that would improve the way girls perceive you, thereby improving your game. You will learn how to decode girls and react to them. However, it really is about how to be good at dating – not just hooking up, how to get a girl-friend, and how to be a good boyfriend.

If you want to have a long-term happy relationship, transforming yourself to be the right guy is the most intelligent thing to do.

You will never fail to impress a girl with the "right guy" attitude. Or better yet, you might even captivate their hearts. So when the time comes when the girl of your dreams arrive, you don't have to worry a lot about impressing her. You will automatically be someone who would be a good partner and you can just focus on getting to know her. It will also save your future relationship from nonsense fights and dramas.

Redefining Relationships

Maybe you found yourself in a park watching every girl pass by and wonder, "Who among them is perfect for me?" Perhaps you have that friend that you like for so long and feel frustrated in getting her attention. This book got the best tricks for you to be in that dream relationship you want.

Romantic relationships are deeper than most people believe. Relationships require commitment and provide personal growth. For the next chapters you'll just not learn the best techniques in impressing a girl. You'll also learn how to grow into the kind of man every girl dreams of having.

Chapter 2 – Preparing To Be the Right Guy

In anything you want to be successful with, you must have a good preparation. A basketball team won't win a championship game if they haven't gone under serious trainings for weeks, months or even years. The same goes with aiming for a successful relationship. You also need to be prepared.

Some dating books or articles may offer you ways or techniques to win a girl for just 2 to 3 weeks. It sounds convincing and effective but it doesn't seem long-lasting. What's the point of dating and impressing the best girl in the world if you're going to lose her in the end? What's the point of experiencing the beauty of her love if it will only last for a few weeks?

Some might be thinking, "At least I experienced it." Well, experiencing it is a good thing, but what if you can have it for the rest of your life? Are you going to lose the chance of being with someone so great just because you aren't prepared?

You see, the real challenge is not really on impressing a girl, but in keeping her. And to be able to keep them, you need to be ready for them. You need to be ready for all her dramas, rants and mood swings as much as you want to be ready for dates, love, care and sex. Of course, it won't be one-sided. Because you are the worth it, and she loves you, she will also deal with your rants, hang-ups and mood swings, and help you get through dark days. And of course, there's sex.

Attraction is natural for anyone to feel. But choices aren't. You have to make her choose you.

And now, here are 5 practical ways you can prepare for being the right guy. Be the "Mr. Right" in this world full of "Mr. Maybes." It's better to be a knight-in-shining-armor-like guy than to be a sluggish one waiting for a girl drop from the sky.

Practice Being Responsible

Responsibility is a big word, and to be fair, this is not about being a good provider. This is about being someone who has "got it together."

Women may love how you look or how you take them to nice dates. But as soon as they find out that you can't keep a job and you don't really have much going, that might make them think twice of staying with you.

Double-check your life if there are areas in your life that you need to be more responsible with. Here is a short checklist of the things you might want to evaluate

- Financial status
- Career
- Relationship status with friends and family
- Emotional Capacity
- Decision making
- Choice of words in communicating

- Physical health

- Personal hygiene

- Anger management

- Habits, attitude and behavior

- Time management

Take one step at a time in improving the following areas in your life. This will not just impress girls; you will also gain personal benefits from it.

Work on yourself

This is related to being responsible; after all, you are responsible for yourself. Work on improving yourself. Take care of your body. Work out and keep yourself well-groomed. Build a decent wardrobe. You don't need to wear suits all the time but you'd need to wear something impressive every once in a while.

Be a Communicator

People love to vent, and women are no exception. Many would agree that women are more vocal when they are upset or emotional about something, although it can be hard to decode what they are upset about. Even though some of their rants are nonsense, they always appreciate it when someone sits with them and simply listen.

Learning to connect with her will make you look like a better man in her eyes. Another plus factor if you can also converse your thoughts and emotions with them. You don't have to be talkative; just trying to communicate with her will increase your chances with her.

Another reason that you should learn to communicate is that for you to understand women better. When they're upset with you (or in some cases they're just depressed), girls tend to be confusing and unpredictable. If you can make her talk even if she said she doesn't want to, the more she'll have trust on you. Women like to talk. Saying they don't want to talk is just their way to say how bad they need you to bear with them.

Know how to speak and listen responsibly. You can practice this with your trusted friends and family. Being open and authentic is actually healthy. It leads to better confidence and maturity.

Know How to Handle Conflicts

Conflicts are natural especially if your relationship is getting deeper. If you want to pursue a strong relationship, you must learn how to handle conflicts. Actually, the best way to handle conflicts is to communicate clearly with an open mind.

Do not try to fight fire with fire. Sometimes, you will have to allow yourself to calm down before you talk to her.

When having arguments, do not use the words "you always do this..." Words like "always" convey that the other person never gets anything right – and that is hurtful. Also, that is a very accusatory tone. Instead, say something like "When you do x, I feel x or "Sometimes, when you x, I start to feel that…"

Have self-control

Cheating is the most common cause of break ups. And cheating is not just a form of temptation. Rather, it is just an outcome of a person's lack of self-control. Any kind of addiction is not healthy because it paralyzes your capacity to gain control over things.

Find out if there are things that are taking far too much of your time that you would be unable to contribute to a relationship. Of course, you should always have your own thing – be that a night out with the boys, or some heavy gaming, but you should always have self-control.

Learn How to Take Charge

It is true that men and women should have equal say in a relationship, but sometimes, a girl would want you to take charge. This doesn't mean that you have to boss her around. It only means that sometimes, she would love it if you would plan dates or even just choose a restaurant. If you are having trouble getting her to agree on something after she says, call her out on it but do not be a jerk about it. Remember that being a good communicator is part of being the "right guy"

Expand Your Creativity

People find creativity sexy. When you take a girl to a date that they have never heard of before, you will surely blow her mind. She will surely talk about it with her friends for days.

And when she talked about it with her friends, she will form an emotional attachment with you. But for you to be able to pull off an impressive date, you need to be creative. You can find hundreds of ideas on Google, but this book also got a few for you. So keep reading.

Girls are not that difficult to understand. Okay, they are. But it's simply because they are the total opposite of men. They do things, see things and believe things that men do not. If you want to be involved in a girl's life, learn to understand them. Therefore, the next chapter will be all about the best ways to decode a girl.

Chapter 3 – Easy Tricks to Decode Girls

If you really want to impress girls and pursue, you should make an effort to understand them. Here are some of the most effective tricks that can help you decode girls better.

Observe Her Body Language

Believe it or not, you can understand girls by looking at the way they move. They are sarcastic creatures and most guys are totally clueless about it. They usually tell you the opposite of what they really think and feel. But if you'll focus more on her movements, you can decode her thoughts better. Observing her body language will also help you tell if she's into you or not. Use this as an advantage to win the girl you really like.

- Watch How She Gazes at You

  If a girl checks you out for more than 3 times, that means she's interested on you. But if she hazes at you for not more than 3 seconds, you didn't get their attention. But don't worry. That is just a sign that you have to make an effort. Approach her. If she makes an eye-contact while you are talking to them, that's a sign of interest. If she keeps on looking at different things, that's a sign that she's bored. If this happens, throw an exciting topic, something that girls really like. If you can talk about fashion and make-up, then go. Do it at your own risk.

- Note How She Touches Her Hair

  You can also tell if a girl is interested on you or not by looking at how she touches her hair. If she plays with her hair, she's totally enjoying your company. But if she jerks it randomly, she's probably thinking how to get out of that conversation with you.

- Look How She Moves Her Hands

When a person is nervous, she reaches out for things to calm herself. It can be her necklace, her bracelet, or any small things nearby. If you notice that she's doing this, you're totally making her heart beat fast. So continue what you're doing. But if she touches things annoyingly like tapping the glass or pressing her fingers on the table, she's most likely irritated or bored.

- Wait Until She Licks Her Lips

  Girls don't lick their lips for no reason, especially if they're talking to men. It's either they want to redirect your attention to her lips or her mouth is too dry because of excitement. Either way, it's a good indication of her interest on you.

- Check her eyebrows.

  No, I'm not telling you to determine if she has nice eyebrows. The thing is, eyebrows can be expressive. Furrowed brows for example may be an indication that she is thinking about something. When she's doing this while you are saying something, it could mean that she's thinking about what you said. If her eyebrows are raised and she is smiling, it could mean that she agrees with you or that she likes what you said or what she's seeing. However, it could be a sign of incredulity if she isn't obviously smiling.

- Check her pupils.

  The pupils dilate when a person is intrigued by you – or what you said. It can be a sign of attraction. If you're in a darker setting like a poorly lit bar or the movies though, it could just be that her eyes needed to adjust to the darkness.

How To React

There is one great subtle trick to impressing a girl using body language and that is *mirroring*.

Mirroring is the art of slightly mimicking another person's actions. For example, when a girl smiles, you smile back. When she glances at the door, you glance at the door. When she drinks wine, you then do so after a few seconds. It's not about doing exactly what she did but doing a version of it in a natural way.

This is especially important when you are dating a girl for the first time, or when you're in the early stages of dating. You see, when you first meet someone, you're quickly trying to measure each other. This is normal and is hardcoded in our DNA. That's how we survived thousands of years ago – by watching behavior.

Mirroring makes another person feel at ease, which makes it an excellent rapport-building tool. Try this during your dates and you'd be amazed at how easy it would be to make connections.

Mine Golden Tips from Ladies' Magazines and Blogs

If you want to learn the habits of women, ladies' magazines are the best place to find them. Girly magazines could reveal to you how some women see relationships. You can get tons of ideas on what actually pleases women.

Girly magazines will tell you the perfect romantic date destinations. It can also teach you women's weaknesses, their communications methods, relationship goals, money habits and more!

Chapter 4 – Walking Your Way To Her Heart

In this chapter you'll find the carefully chosen techniques that will not just impress girls but also make a strong foundation for a relationship with a girl.

Plan Ahead

Before you start looking for someone to date, make it clear to yourself why you want to date someone. Is it because you're ready for commitment? Or you're just longing to be with someone amazing? If it's not yet clear to you why, it would be better if you think about it first. No one wants to be with an unsure person. But if your motives are already clear to you, you can now plan out how you're going to make your move.

- **Are You Ready?**

Ask yourself this: what kind of woman do you want to date? Try creating an ideal girl. But this doesn't mean you're going to go after a girl who resembles exactly your ideal one. It's a waste of time if you will just aimlessly look for a girl

Make sure that you are practicing the "right guy" attitude. You may impress a girl with your words and looks but that wouldn't make them choose you. Again, attraction is natural; choice isn't. Make her choose you by being the right guy.

- **Are the Things You Need Ready?**

  Make sure you got everything you need in dating a girl: time, money, effort and ideas. Oh, you should also bring with you some love, patience and understanding, too. They're important. Don't forget that.

First, prepare a 1-minute introduction or 1-2 sentences about yourself. That way, you can have a clever answer to the standard question of "so what can you tell me about yourself?" This way, you'll be more confident when you do need to tell someone about yourself.

Do your homework. You can try to get the attention of a girl try making some research on what's trending today. That's always a safe topic. You can also prepare a list of conversation topics and practice it before the date so you won't be as nervous when the time comes.

There is a full-proof way to maintain conversation though – just keep her talking. People love talking about themselves so ask her about what she's been up to and then ask follow up questions.

- This way you will have many things to say when you talked to the girl you want to impress.

Get Her Attention

There are many ways that you can get the attention of a girl without being annoying or creepy. You can start by just saying "Hey." Don't listen to pick up artists trying to sell you ideas on clever things you can say to get a girl's attention. Good old "hey" is neutral and any decent person would reply to that.

You can start by asking friendly questions like, "Do you know _____?" You can also open a light discussion like "Hey, you remind me of _____" or "Have you heard the news about _____"

Don't be afraid to talk. Anyone could appreciate a good conversation. But don't forget to observe if they're getting bored already. Take note of her body language (mentioned in chapter 3). If she's getting bored, get her to talk about herself. Crack jokes, but never do mean jokes.

- **Be Real**

  Don't forget to be your natural self, too. Be authentic. Revel in what you are. For example, if you are naturally awkward, you can just try self-effacing humor instead of pretending that you are such a suave guy. If you are into film, allow yourself to gush all about the latest movie from Tarantino. If the girl sees your genuineness, she'd respond positively. At least, girls who are worth it would. Also, people love it when you show who you are and what you are passionate about, so just do you.

- **Be confident**

  Also, wear confidence. Be confident about who you are as a man, and girls will surely notice you. A vital aspect of confidence is knowing that you are well-groomed though. You don't have to dress like Don Draper. Clean men can outshine good looks. Clean men are always attractive, *and sexy*.

- **Get Her Number and Social Media Account**

  Once you felt that the girl is already comfortable with you, you may ask for her phone number or social media account. But don't be obvious about your intention. Wait for it to come naturally in the conversation. Then, talk more as you succeeded in getting her number.

- **Build Friendship**

  Text her the next day after you got your number. Although it's tempting to flirt with her, just start with the friendly approach. Flirting is fun but it's best to build some friendliness first. Share some clean jokes with her. Tell her something funny or interesting you encountered on the way to work and watch how she reacts.

Don't worry about the "friend-zoned" label. There is no such thing about nice guys being constantly friend-zoned and unable to become a romantic interest. If a girl is interested with you, she's interested in you and that's it. She won't convince herself otherwise just because you're her "friend." Just focus first on building strong foundations. Remember that the connection is important.

- **Make Emotional Talks**

  As your friendship grows, try making emotional talks from time to time. Small talks can be boring so try opening up things that involve feelings and emotions. This will make her attachment to you even stronger. Emotional talks are deep, so when you get to talk to her this way, you're creating a deeper relationship. Ask her some of her emotional experience and make her feel like you're really listening and understanding.

- **Show vulnerability**

  You can also open emotional topics about you. Don't be afraid to be vulnerable to her. Real men are vulnerable. Show her that you can also feel. This will make her connect to you more.

- **Just be there for her**

  There will come a point when she just really needs someone to tell her everything will be ok. Be that person

- **Be consistent**

  Be reliable. There is no need for mind games if you are really after a relationship.

- **Don't be clingy**

  Do not come on too strong. Do not be too needy and get angry when she decides to go out with someone else or do the things she likes. If you want to take things to the next level, then you need to tell her how you feel, which is what we'll discuss ion the next section,

How To Tell Her What You Feel

Of course, you'll only do this when you've been dating for a while and you perhaps want to just let her know how special she is, or if you want to go exclusive. Just remember to be natural and be true about your feelings. Make it clear to her that you want something greater than friendship.

Tell her how you find her amazing and how she's invading your mind lately. Tell her how you want to pursue a relationship with her. Don't rush her. Give her time to think about it. Tell her that you're willing to wait for her response.

Chapter 5 – Romantic Date Ideas to Captivate Her Heart

When a girl approved your invitation for a date, make sure to give your best. Make this one of the most memorable day (or night) of her life. But before you take a girl out for a romantic date, remember the dos and don'ts first:

- Pick her up from her house.

- Say something nice about her but don't overdo it.

- Just relax and maintain good conversation

- Make eye contact

- Drive her home after the date.

- Don't go after a kiss. Settle for a good hug first.

- Ask for a second date.

Remember that the first date is one of the most important key of winning the girl you want. You have to do everything to consider you to be her partner. This is your chance to show her that you are someone worth keeping and pursuing. So do everything you can to set up a creative date. But if you are short of ideas right now, here are 5 fantastic first date idea that can surely impress a girl.

Bring her to a street fair or a food festival.

The standard lunch date can be boring and if you're an awkward person, you might have a hard time maintaining conversation while eating. Why not enjoy food someplace where you can do something else, like in a food festival? Even just bringing her to the food truck center or a weekly farmers' market and experiment on homemade hot-sauces might prove to be fun. You can walk around while nibbling on finger food and try a range of unique food. You can then find out how cool she is when she jokes about diarrhea or gas within 24 hours of meeting you.

Go on a road trip

Road trips are fun and the best thing is, you only need gas money and some money for gas station food! Google the interesting places near your town and plan your road trip ahead. You can even memorize some trivia. That way, you can have something to say while driving too. Prepare a good road trip playlist to set the atmosphere. Troll for any photo booth you'll find along the way. Take pictures and keep them as remembrance of every place you've been to. Bring some finger food.

More than a Movie Night

Look for a drive-in. Take some popcorn, fries or box of chocolates and relax with her. You can then engage in a post-movie discussion, if the movie is good, or just poke fun at the film, if it's atrocious.

A walk in the park

Head to a park or playground and simply enjoy the moment. Go people watching and play a game of create-this-person's backstory. Find out how she views people. You can also head on a perfect place to wait for the sunset. While waiting for the sunrise, try talking about goals and dreams.

Amusement Park

Amusement parks are fun! Try as many rides and you want and do not be afraid to look silly.

Try the foods available there and exchange energetic conversations. Take a lot of pictures of one another. You can also take beautiful candid shots of her and give her a copy. She will surely appreciate that.

Conclusion

Although this book has presented the best tips about dating and impressing a girl, there is no guarantee that she'll choose you. No one has the control over her choices so always be ready for whatever decision she'll make. Rejection won't make you less than a man. It will just teach more of the value of dating and relationships.

If she decided to step a level higher, then that would be great! Just remember to always be the "right guy" and always prioritize to understand girls more than anything else.

Thank you again for purchasing this book!

Finally, if you enjoyed this book, then I'd like to ask you for a favor, would you be kind enough to leave a review for this book on Amazon? It'd be greatly appreciated!

Click here to leave a review for this book on Amazon!

Thank you and good luck!

Check Out My Other Book

Below you will find some of my other popular books that are popular on Amazon and Kindle as well. Simply click on the links below to check them out. Alternatively, you can visit my author page on Amazon to see other work done by me. If the links do not work, for whatever reason, you can simply search for these titles on the Amazon website to find them.

The Ultimate Guide To Meet And Marry The Women Of Your Dreams: How To Find Your Life Partner And Soul Mate

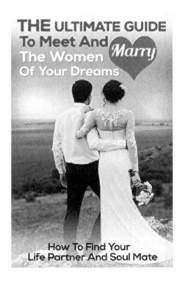

Click here to check out 'The Ultimate Guide To Meet And Marry The Women

Of Your Dreams: How To Find Your Life Partner And Soul Mate' book.

Or go to: http://amzn.to/28QjV26

Before You Go

If you liked this book, you may like these other books from George K.

Check out more books from George K.

Visit :

http://www.amazon.com/George-K./e/B00KU46WW6

Made in the USA
Las Vegas, NV
23 December 2020

14570922R00028